BRITISH MUSEUM

Fun Book

ANCIENT ROME

Sandy Ransford
Illustrated by David Farris

BRITISH MUSEUM ⛫ PRESS

Published by British Museum Press
A division of The British Museum Company Ltd
46 Bloomsbury Street, London WC1B 3QQ

ISBN 0 7141 2169 X
A catalogue record for this book is available from the British Library

Designed and illustrated by David Farris
Cover design by David Farris
Printed in Great Britain by Page Bros, Norwich

Contents

CAN YOU TELL ME WHEN ROME WAS BUILT?

AT NIGHT.

WHAT MAKES YOU SAY THAT?

BECAUSE MUM'S ALWAYS SAYING ROME WASN'T BUILT IN A DAY.

Introduction

Rome was the greatest city in the ancient world. According to legend it was founded in 753 BC by Romulus and Remus, twin sons of the god Mars, and its influence lasted for over 1,000 years. The Roman civilization gave the world great law-makers, writers, military leaders, engineers and architects. To the Romans we owe many of our roads, laws, and weights and measures systems. Even much of our language is derived from Latin. But this great civilization that ruled Europe, Asia Minor, North Africa and the Near East, and gave the world communications, plumbing and heating systems not equalled for almost 2,000 years, was also brutal, bloody and immensely cruel. All the hard work, and much of the fighting in the amphitheatres, was done by slaves, who had no human rights. The Colosseum in Rome was built for the killing of men and of animals – in one spectacle alone 2,000 gladiators and 230 wild animals were scheduled to die. In the later years Christians were tortured and put to death there. The emperors wielded supreme power, but even they could not escape the bloodshed. Of the first twelve emperors, four were assassinated, two committed suicide, one was poisoned and one was suffocated.

It is this astonishing contrast between civilization and barbarism that makes ancient Rome so fascinating – and this book is a collection of puzzles and jokes based upon it. There are quizzes, crosswords and word-searches; number puzzles and mystifying mind-benders; mazes and other tantalizing picture puzzles – even an ancient game to play. And if you get stuck, you can have a good laugh at the ancient Roman jokes scattered around. The checklist opposite should help if you don't know much about ancient Rome.

Spero libet!

The Roman republic lasted from 509 BC until 27 BC and the empire from 27 BC until AD 476, when Odoacer, leader of the German armies, became king of Italy.

Some famous Romans

Julius Caesar - military leader and politician - visited Britain around 55 BC and was murdered in 44 BC by Brutus and other conspirators.

Writers

Cicero
(also an orator and statesman)
Catullus (poet)
Horace (poet)
Juvenal (poet)
Livy (historian)
Ovid (poet)
Seneca
(philosopher and dramatist)
Suetonius (biographer)
Tacitus (historian)
Virgil
(poet who wrote *Aeneid*)

> WHY IS HISTORY THE SWEETEST LESSON?

> IT'S FULL OF DATES.

Emperors

Augustus 31 BC to AD 14
Tiberius AD 14-37
Caligula AD 37-41
Claudius AD 41-54
Nero AD 54-68
Trajan AD 98-117 (whose column still exists in Rome)
Hadrian AD 117-138 (who built the wall across northern Britain)
Antoninus Pius AD 138-161 (who built a turf wall across Scotland from the Forth to the Clyde)
Septimius Severus AD 193-211 (who built the famous arch that still exists in the Forum in Rome)
Caracalla AD 211-217 (whose baths still exist in Rome)
Constantine AD 307-337 (the first Christian emperor, who founded Constantinople)

How well do you know the Roman numerals? Can you work out the answers to these sums?

1 X - IX =

2 IV × III =

3 V + VI - IV =

4 XX ÷ IV =

5 XVIII ÷ VI =

6 L - XXV =

7 M + C + L + X - V =

8 XIV - VII + III ÷ II =

9 D - CC =

10 XC - LXXX =

WHAT WAS THE ROMAN FORUM?

ER, A TWO-UM PLUS A TWO-UM?

How many differences can you spot between these two pictures of the Roman forum?

In the Colosseum

In the Colosseum gladiators fought bloody battles with each other and with wild animals like lions and leopards. There were different kinds of gladiators, such as the *hoplomachus*, who was heavily armed; the *retiarius*, who fought with a trident and a net; the *secutor*, who chased the *retiarius*; the *myrmillo*, who had a symbol of a fish on his helmet; and the *bestiarius*, who fought wild animals. Can you solve these puzzles about them?

1   The organizer of the games divided his gladiators into five groups: hoplomachae, retiarii, secutori, myrmillii and bestiarii. There were equal numbers of hoplomachae and myrmillii, and twice as many retiarii as hoplomachae. The number of secutori was halfway between the numbers of hoplomachae and retiarii. The number of bestiarii equalled the total number of hoplomachae and secutori. Altogether there were 800 gladiators. How many of each kind were there?

2.   Thursday was a bad day for a certain number of top-class gladiators in the amphitheatre. In the first round, half a gladiator more than half the squad were killed. In the second round, half a gladiator more than half the remainder died. In the third round, half a gladiator more than half of what was left died, and in the fourth round, the remaining gladiator was killed. How many were there in this top-class gladiator squad?

3.   Another supreme squad consisted of a certain number of gladiators. If you add six to that number, then divide it by ten, the result would be the same as if you had subtracted four and divided by eight. How many were in the squad?

Which two gladiators pictured below are exactly the same?

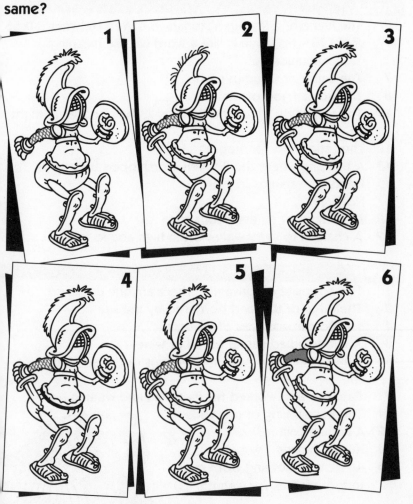

Crossword Primus

Across

2 The name of a Roman historian who lived between AD 55 and 120 – his name is like a word we use meaning 'uncommunicative' *(7)*

7 The Emperor Claudius's wife *(9)*

8 The Roman god of war *(4)*

10 The means by which the Romans lit their houses at night *(3-4)*

12 The Latin word for 'house' *(5)*

13 A building where the Romans worshipped their gods *(6)*

15 Fleets of warships *(6)*

17 Not well *(3)*

18 The colour of an emperor's toga *(6)*

19 A channel to carry water, often high above the ground *(8)*

Down

1 The opposite of 'private' - where anyone could go *(6)*

3 The edge of the land bordered by the sea *(5)*

4 The Roman goddess of wisdom *(7)*

5 A two-handled vessel for oil or wine *(7)*

6 Public spectacles held in the circus or the amphitheatre *(5)*

9 Captives who worked for free men and women *(6)*

11 The Roman king of the gods *(7)*

12 A Roman coin *(8)*

14 Human beings *(6)*

16 An item of clothing worn over indoor clothes for warmth *(5)*

CAN YOU TELL ME THE WAY TO BATH?

PERSONALLY, I ALWAYS USE SOAP AND HOT WATER.

11

Emperors All

See how much you know about the Roman emperors with this testing quiz.

1. Who was the first Roman emperor?
2. Who was his successor after 45 years?
3. Which emperor threatened to make his horse, Incitatus, a consul?
4. Which emperor's name meant 'little boot'?
5. Which emperor built the great baths that can still be seen in Rome?
6. Which emperor built a wall across northern Britain from Wallsend-on-Tyne to Bowness on the Solway Firth?
7. And who built another wall further north?
8. Which emperor 'fiddled' (or, more likely, sang) while Rome burnt in AD 64?
9. Who was the first Christian emperor?
10. Which of these people was *not* an emperor: Valerian, Suetonius, Otho?

WHEN IS A PIECE OF WOOD LIKE AN EMPEROR?

WHEN IT'S MADE INTO A RULER.

Odd Emperor Out

Which of these statues of the Emperor Augustus is the odd one out?

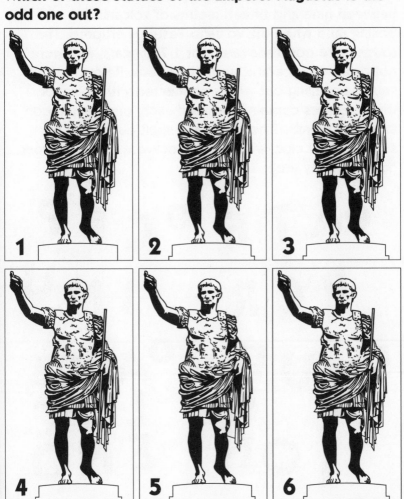

Mountains of Fire

In AD 79 Pompeii and Herculaneum were buried under between nine and fifteen metres of volcanic ash and boiling mud when the volcano Vesuvius erupted. The towns were not discovered for 1,700 years, and were not properly excavated until the 1860s. Below are four squares spelling out words connected with volcanoes: three squares contain one word each; one square contains two words. The words are spelt out round the square either clockwise or anticlockwise. Can you work out what they are?

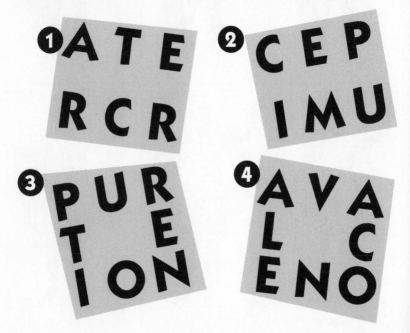

Puzzling Pompeii

Can you find your way through the maze of streets and buildings from Vesuvius to the sea?

Imperator!

'Imperator' was the title given to a Roman commander by his soldiers after a victory in battle, and it became part of the imperial title of the emperors. The names of all the Roman emperors listed below can be traced out in the grid opposite. The words may read across, up, down or diagonally, either forwards or backwards, but they are all in straight lines.

ANTONINUS PIUS (2 lines)	**MARCUS AURELIUS** (2 lines)
AUGUSTUS	**NERO**
CALIGULA	**PROBUS**
CARACALLA	**SEPTIMIUS SEVERUS** (2 lines)
CLAUDIUS	
CONSTANTINE	**THEODOSIUS**
DIOCLETIAN	**TIBERIUS**
GALBA	**TITUS**
GETA	**TRAJAN**
HADRIAN	**VESPASIAN**
LUCIUS VERUS (2 lines)	**VITELLIUS**

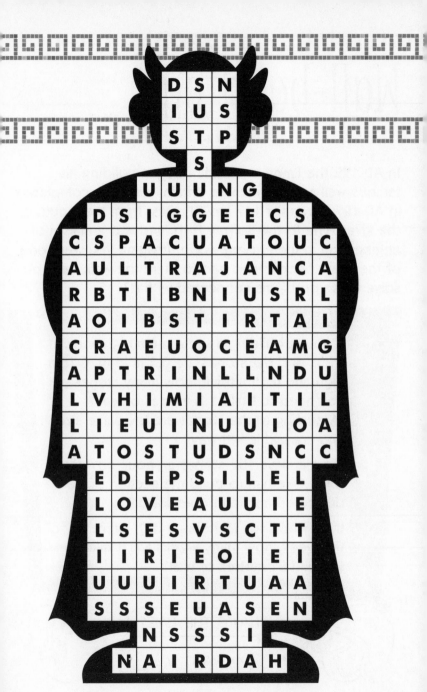

Wall-building

In AD 122 the Emperor Hadrian began building his famous wall across northern Britain, which he completed in AD 127. It ran for 117 km/73 miles, from the mouth of the River Tyne to the Solway Firth, and was a marvel of engineering in the ancient world. Imagine you were one of the many people who had to build the wall. Can you solve these problems connected with it?

1 If you're building a section 6m high and 3m wide, and the stones are 0.3 m long, 0.15m high and 0.15m thick, how many stones will you need to build 1.5 metres of wall? (Assuming all the stones are the same size and are laid lengthways.)

2 If a man lays 150 stones an hour, how long will it take him to build the section of wall described above in question 1?

3 If he works for 12 hours a day, every day of the week, how many weeks will it take him to build 21 metres of wall?

WHAT'S THE TIME?

XX PAST IV.

The top picture shows a fort on Hadrian's wall. The lower pictures show the same image reversed. Only one of them shows the correct image. Which picture is it?

(1)

(2)

(3)

(4)

Among the Gods

Do you know the names of the Roman gods and what they stood for? See if you can match them up.

Gods' names	Gods of
Apollo	king of the gods
Ceres	home life
Diana	war
Juno	fire and smithing
Jupiter	sea
Mars	sun
Mercury	crop-growing
Neptune	hunting
Pluto	queen of the gods
Venus	messenger of the gods
Vesta	underworld
Vulcan	love

Gods Squared

Two of the squares of this picture of Jupiter are exactly the same – can you spot which ones they are?

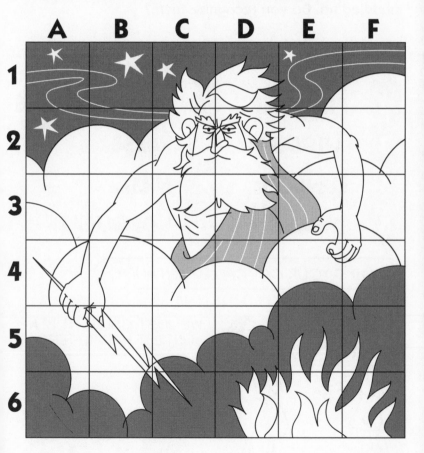

Word Muddle

Below are ten words you will come across when reading about ancient Rome, but their letters have been muddled up. Do you recognize them?

1 RACESA	**6** EBLANIPE
2 PREROME	**7** TRAMPTHEHIAE
3 NICTARPIA	**8** VALSE
4 LUNSCO	**9** NILTA
5 TREASON	**10** UDEQUCAT

WHY'S YOUR CAT CALLED BEN HUR?

WE JUST CALLED IT BEN UNTIL IT HAD KITTENS.

In this chaotic chariot racing scene, how many horses, how many chariots and how many charioteers are there?

Crossword Secundus

YES, SECUNDUS MEANS 'SECOND'.

Across

1 See 6 Down
3 The Mediterranean - - - laps the coast of Italy *(3)*
4 A row of columns, such as you find at a temple *(9)*
7 This dynasty of emperors reigned from AD 69 to 96 *(7)*
8 Gladiators fought wild ones in the amphitheatres *(6)*
9 The total to which things add up *(6)*
10 The city which was the centre of the Roman civilization *(4)*
12 The emperor who reigned from AD 54 to 68 *(4)*
13 A curved stone structure *(4)*
15 The commander of 100 men in the Roman army *(9)*
16 Cleaned in water *(6)*

Down

1 Armour that protected the legs *(7)*
2 For example, 15 March 44 BC *(4)*
3 A Roman politician *(7)*
5 The day Julius Caesar was assassinated *(4, 2, 5)*
6 and *1 Across* A brigade of soldiers who protected the emperor *(10, 5)*
10 With Remus, one of the mythical founders of Rome *(7)*
11 One of Julius Caesar's murderers *(6)*
14 Four-legged means of transport *(5)*

24

Bath Time

The words in italic type are the names of different parts of a typical Roman baths. Can you match them up with the words in ordinary type, which explain what they are?

1 *Caldarium*
2 *Tepidarium*
3 *Frigidarium*
4 *Apodyterium*
5 *Palaestra*
6 *Hypocaust*
7 *Labrum*
8 *Alveus*

a **Bath**
b **Open exercise area**
c **Hot room**
d **Warm room**
e **Cold plunge bath**
f **Changing room**
g **Heating system**
h **Shallow wash basin**

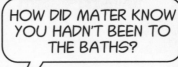

HOW DID MATER KNOW YOU HADN'T BEEN TO THE BATHS?

I FORGOT TO WET THE TOWEL.

Look at these six little pictures of a Roman baths. One thing has been added (a different thing each time) to pictures 2 to 6. Can you spot what they are?

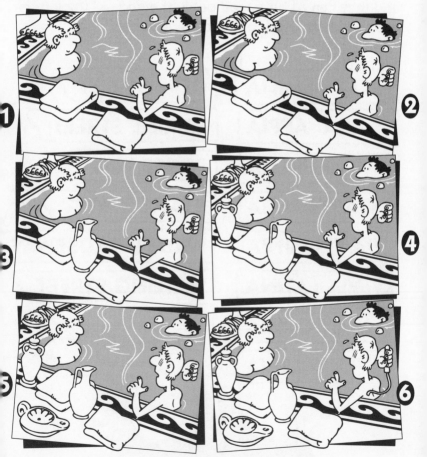

Via Wherea?

Roman roads are supposed to run in straight lines but the names of those in this puzzle snake up and down, forwards and backwards. The names are listed below and they can all be traced out in the grid. All the letters in the grid are used, but each is used only once.

VIA AEMILIA

VIA APPIA

VIA AURELIA

VIA EGNATIA

VIA FLAMINIA

VIA LATINA

VIA POPILIA

VIA VALERIA

DERE STREET

ERMINE STREET

FOSSE WAY

STANE STREET

WADE'S CAUSEWAY

WATLING STREET

T

Y	W	A	T	R	E	E	F	T	E	E	R
A	W	T	S	A	W	S	O	N	E	S	T
S	E	L	G	Y	E	S	M	I	V	A	V
U	A	I	N	S	T	A	R	A	I	I	I
S	C	W	T	R	T	N	E	A	I	L	A
E	D	A	E	E	S	E	T	E	M	P	A
L	E	A	D	E	S	E	E	A	L	P	I
A	R	I	E	R	T	R	I	M	F	V	A
V	A	I	V	V	A	I	N	I	A	I	A
O	P	I	A	I	A	G	N	V	A	U	A
P	I	L	N	I	L	E	A	T	I	R	E
A	I	V	A	T	A	A	I	V	A	I	L

WHY DID THE ROMANS
BUILD STRAIGHT ROADS?

SO THE ANCIENT BRITONS
COULDN'T HIDE
ROUND THE CORNERS.

29

Travelling Problems

1 The Roman legions marched many hundreds of miles along the Empire's excellent roads. The city of Naples is about 48 miles from Beneventum. If Legion A sets out from Naples at 8 a.m. and marches at 4 m.p.h. heading for Beneventum, and Legion B sets out from Beneventum at 6 a.m. and marches at 3 m.p.h. heading for Naples, at what time will each legion arrive at its destination?

2 On one of its marches a legion encountered a river 20m wide. So, of course, they built a bridge across it. If the bridge's span equals the river's plus one quarter on the south bank and one fifth on the north bank, what is the total length of the bridge?

3 The commander of one legion, of 1,000 men, had a problem. Each month, probably because he worked them too hard, or marched them too hard, ten per cent of his men disappeared. They ran off with their armour and weapons and simply vanished, never to be seen again. If this situation continued for a year, how many men would he have left? (You'll need a pencil and a piece of paper to work this out.)

On the March

These soldiers are marching off to defend the borders of the empire against invaders. How many things can you spot wrong with the picture?

Hic, Haec, Hoc

This is a very old game for two people (the three Latin words of the title all mean 'this') which was played all over the world, including in Rome. It's very simple, you can play it anywhere and all you need are your own hands! It is sometimes called 'Scissors, Paper, Stone' and this is how you play it.

Three different positions of your hands indicate the three different things: scissors, paper and stone. Two fingers in a V-shape (no rude gestures!) are used to indicate scissors. A flat, open hand with the fingers together indicates paper, and a clenched fist indicates stone. The two players hide their hands behind their backs and form one hand into one of the three shapes. As they do so, they chant 'Hic, haec, hoc', and on the third word each shows their hand in its chosen shape to the other player. If the hands are in different positions, one player will win according to these rules: scissors cut paper, so a V-shaped hand beats a flat, open hand; paper can wrap stone, so an open hand beats a clenched fist; stone blunts scissors, so a clenched fist beats a V-shape. If the players' hands are in the same position, then it is a draw and they must play again.

Play can be fast and furious and the winner of each round gains a point. The winner is the player who has gained the most points after an agreed number of rounds.

On the Ides (15th) of March 44 BC, Julius Caesar was stabbed to death by a gang of conspirators led by Brutus. The top picture shows the scene. The pictures below are all negative images of the one above, but only one is correct. Which one is it?

Roman Writers

Can you recognize the names of these Roman writers from alternate letters of their names?

1	L - V -
2	C - C - R -
3	H - R - C -
4	V - R - I -
5	O - I -
6	J - V - N - L
7	S - N - C -
8	P - A - T - S
9	C - T - L - U -
10	P - T - O - I - S
11	S - E - O - I - S
12	T - C - T - S

AND WHAT'S YOUR NEW PLAY CALLED, DEAR?

I CALLED IT 'JULIUS, GRAB THE GIRL QUICKLY BEFORE SHE RUNS AWAY'.

THAT'S A VERY LONG TITLE. WHY DON'T YOU JUST CALL IT 'JULIUS, SEIZE HER'?

The Romans were fond of going to the theatre, where the actors wore masks to show the kind of character they were portraying: comic characters had upturned, grinning mouths and tragic characters had gaping, drooping mouths. How many comic and how many tragic masks can you spot in the picture?

We met the different kinds of gladiators earlier. Here you have to see how many of each kind you can find hidden in the grid opposite. The words may run across, up, down or diagonally, either forwards or backwards, but they are all in straight lines. To remind you, the names are:

MYRMILLO

RETIARIUS

BESTIARIUS

SECUTOR

HOPLOMACHUS

WHO ARE THE ONLY PEOPLE THE CAESARS HAVE TO TAKE THEIR LAUREL CROWNS OFF TO?

THEIR BARBERS.

M	O	L	P	O	H	O	P	L	O	M	A
Y	H	O	P	L	O	M	A	C	H	U	S
B	O	R	H	O	P	L	M	S	M	R	U
E	P	U	O	L	L	I	M	U	Y	M	I
S	L	C	T	R	O	R	S	I	R	M	R
T	O	E	H	Y	M	R	M	R	M	Y	A
I	M	S	O	M	A	O	S	A	I	R	I
S	A	U	P	R	C	T	E	I	L	M	T
U	C	I	L	E	H	U	S	T	L	I	E
I	H	R	O	T	U	C	E	S	O	M	R
R	U	A	M	I	S	E	C	E	M	Y	R
A	S	I	A	A	E	S	U	B	Y	R	O
I	E	T	C	R	C	U	T	O	R	M	T
T	C	E	H	I	U	T	O	L	M	I	U
S	U	R	U	U	T	Y	R	L	I	L	C
E	T	R	S	S	O	M	M	I	L	L	E
B	O	Y	M	Y	R	M	I	L	L	O	S

True or False?

How many of the following statements are true and how many are false?

1	In the third century BC Rome controlled the whole of Italy, and its empire continued until the fifth century AD.
2	Julius Caesar was the first Roman emperor.
3	The Roman name for York was Mancunium.
4	A sistrum was a musical instrument like a rattle.
5	Pots were placed at street corners to collect urine, which was used in cloth-making.
6	A silvarius was a Roman silver coin.
7	The Romans used a system of hot air central heating.
8	The Romans played a game similar to bowling.
9	The Romans didn't bake bread as they had no ovens.
10	A *lararium* was a shrine to the household gods.
11	The Romans ate dormice.
12	The *triclinium* was a bedroom in a Roman house.

Stone Pictures

A mosaic is a picture made of lots of tiny stones. How many differences can you spot between the two mosaics below?

Crossword Tertius

YES, 'THIRD'.

Across

5 The name of the formation of soldiers who overlapped their shields to form a tortoise-like shape *(7)*

7 Robe worn by male Roman citizens *(4)*

9 The name of the fortification built across northern Britain by a Roman emperor *(8, 4)*

10 The emperor who threatened to make his horse a consul *(8)*

13 Outside *(8)*

15 Kind of Roman footwear *(6)*

17 Member of a tribe that eventually overthrew the Romans *(8)*

Down

1 You walk through this when you enter a building *(7)*

2 You may walk up or down this *(5)*

3 Much of ancient Rome's buildings today are in - - - - *(5)*

4 A picture made of many tiny stones *(6)*

6 Someone you don't know *(8)*

8 A Roman house *(5)*

11 The Romans' language *(5)*

12 The courtyard and reception area of a Roman house *(6)*

14 A narrow bit of the sea going inland *(5)*

15 A large boat *(4)*

16 Household pet or guard animal *(3)*

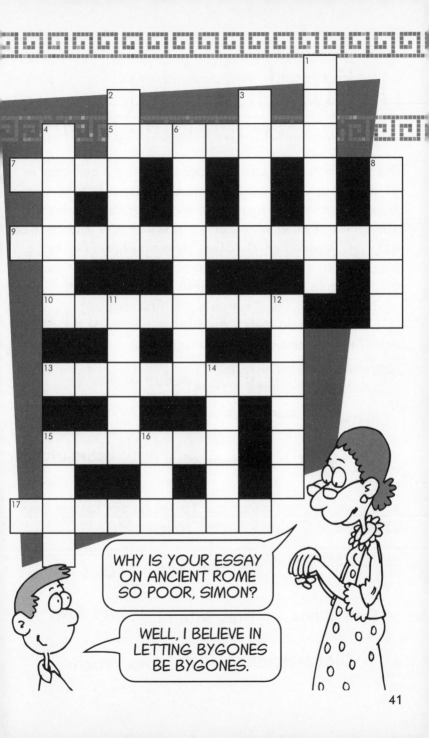

WHY IS YOUR ESSAY ON ANCIENT ROME SO POOR, SIMON?

WELL, I BELIEVE IN LETTING BYGONES BE BYGONES.

Julian Calendar

Did you know that Julius Caesar instituted a calendar in 46 BC which was used throughout western Europe until Pope Gregory XIII introduced the Gregorian calendar in 1582? The Roman year started in March and four of their months: September, October, November and December had the same names as we know them by. (Their names meant the seventh, eighth, ninth and tenth months, which makes sense if March is the first month.)

Can you match the Roman names of the other months with their English counterparts?

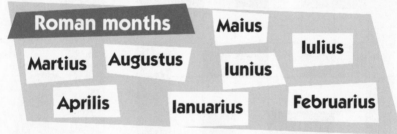

Roman months

Maius
Iulius
Martius
Augustus
Iunius
Aprilis
Ianuarius
Februarius

And then can you match the Roman names for the days of the week with their English counterparts?

Roman days

Dies Solis
Dies Martis
Dies Lunae
Dies Saturni
Dies Jovis
Dies Mercurii
Dies Veneris

The Romans used sundials to measure time. How many
of those our artist has drawn are exactly the same?

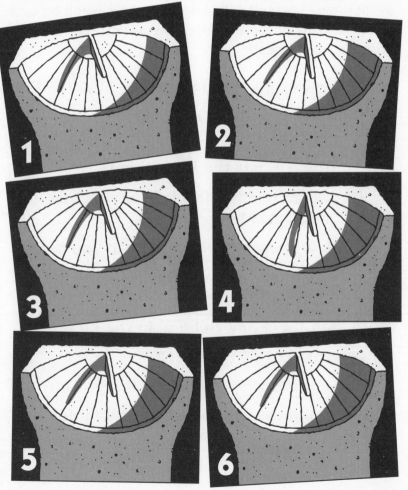

Housey, Housey

Here's a puzzle to test your memory. Study the diagram of a Roman house on the opposite page for just half a minute (time yourself with a watch) then cover it up and see how many of the questions below you can answer about it. Don't cheat!

1   How many columns has the peristyle?

2   How many people are there in the picture?

3   Which way is the lady facing?

4   Are there any animals in the picture, and if so, what are they?

5   How many pointed trees can you see?

6   Which upstairs window has someone looking from it?

7   Are there any children in the picture?

8   What covers the roof?

9   How many windows face the garden?

10   How many vessels are on the table?

Summing Up

Here's another chance to test your knowledge of Roman numerals. Are the sums below correct? If any of them aren't, do you know what the correct answers should be?

1	XV ÷ V = IV
2	VIII + XIII = XXII
3	D ÷ C = V
4	IV + VI ÷ II = X
5	C x LX = DC
6	XVIII ÷ III = VI
7	XIX - IV ÷ V = IV
8	XX + XL = LD
9	V + IV + XI = XX
10	IX x III = XXVIII

. . . and how many things beginning with the letter E can you spot in the picture?

$E=MC^2$

In

Out

What's in a Name?

Can you match the Roman names of these British towns and cities with their modern counterparts?

Roman	Modern
Aqua Arnemetiae	Winchester
Aquae Sulis	Carmarthen
Camulodunum	Chester
Corinium	Bath
Devana Castra	Buxton
Durnovaria	Carlisle
Durovernum	Colchester
Lindum	Cirencester
Londinium	Canterbury
Luguvallum	St Albans
Maridunum	Lincoln
Ratae	London
Venta Belgarum	Leicester
Verulanium	Dorchester

Founders of Rome

According to legend, Rome was founded by the twin sons of Mars, Romulus and Remus, who were abandoned as babies but rescued and brought up by a she-wolf. Which of the pictures of them below is different from all the others and why?

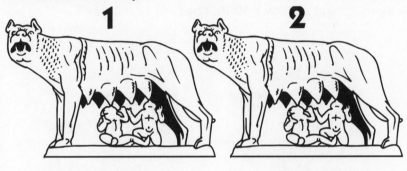

WHAT ANIMAL DID A ROMAN LOOK LIKE WHEN HE WAS IN THE BATHS?

A LITTLE BEAR.

All That Remains . . .

There are Roman remains at lots of places in Britain, and listed below are just some of them. All the words can be traced out in the grid opposite. They may read across, up, down or diagonally, either forwards or backwards, but they are all in straight lines. Do you know why so many of the names end in 'chester' or 'cester'?

BATH
BIGNOR
CAERNARFON
CAERWENT
CANTERBURY
CARMARTHEN
CHESTER
CHICHESTER
CIRENCESTER
COLCHESTER
DORCHESTER
EXETER
FISHBOURNE
LANCASTER

LEICESTER
LINCOLN
LONDON
LULLINGSTONE
NEATH
NEWPORT
PEVENSEY
PORTCHESTER
ROCHESTER
SILCHESTER
ST ALBANS
WINCHESTER
WROXETER
YORK

C	H	I	C	H	E	S	T	E	R	T	L	L
I	O	B	C	N	N	L	O	C	N	I	L	A
R	L	L	B	I	G	N	O	R	F	E	O	N
E	J	U	C	C	N	D	C	N	I	O	N	C
N	K	L	N	H	M	K	H	C	S	J	D	A
C	K	L	D	N	E	T	E	P	H	K	O	S
E	R	I	C	J	A	S	S	E	B	L	N	T
S	O	N	A	B	T	I	T	V	O	R	S	E
T	Y	G	E	E	C	L	E	E	U	E	T	R
E	R	S	R	T	A	C	R	N	R	T	A	E
R	U	T	N	R	R	H	P	S	N	S	L	T
E	B	O	A	O	M	E	Q	E	E	E	B	S
T	R	N	R	P	A	S	T	Y	R	H	A	E
S	E	E	F	W	R	T	N	E	S	C	N	H
E	T	T	O	E	T	E	E	X	X	R	S	C
H	N	V	N	N	H	R	A	E	W	O	X	N
C	A	E	R	W	E	N	T	T	Y	D	R	I
O	C	Z	K	J	N	N	H	E	D	G	P	W
R	E	T	S	E	H	C	T	R	O	P	W	R

Ladies' Day

1. A Roman lady, who was shy of revealing her true age, replied that she was 35 years old, not counting Saturdays and Sundays, when her nephew asked her how old she was. How old was she really?

2. Another Roman lady had a collection of beautiful little mirrors. All but two of them were gold, all but two of them were silver and all but two of them were bronze. How many mirrors were in her collection?

3. A third Roman lady sent one of her household slaves out to buy olive oil and wine. If, together, they cost the modern-day equivalent of £11 and the wine cost £10 more than the olive oil, what was the price of each?

IS IT TRUE THAT YOU CAN'T STOP TIME?

I'M NOT SURE. MY SISTER WENT TO SEE HER FRIEND THIS MORNING AND STOPPED HOURS.

All Underground

The catacombs are a complex of underground chambers and passageways in Rome where the early Christians met to avoid persecution, and where many were buried. They are easy to get lost in. Can you find your way through our picture of them, out into the daylight?

Muddled Sentences

The words in these sentences are in the wrong order. Can you sort them out and make sense of them?

1. Its power founded in 753 BC was Rome and lasted AD 476 until.

2. To measure the Romans weight the pound the ounce *libra* and *uncia* used.

3. Continued in the Republic was set up until 509 BC and Roman the first century BC.

4. Caesar Roman collapsed killed Julius the Republic when was.

5. The month days of the main three Roman the Calends the Nones were and the Ides.

6. Rome in AD 410 sacked Alaric the Visigoth.

7. Of Pompeii at the ruins vineyards have remains been among found the.

8. Swimming bathers entering a footbath walked through the Roman pool before.

9. *Dolia* Roman pots large earthenware shops had counters called set into their.

10. Bronze or Roman cooking earthenware utensils were made of.

Donkey Work

These three Roman boys are leading their donkeys out to work, but the donkeys got rather frisky and their lead ropes got tangled up. Can you work out which boy is leading which donkey?

Marcus

Ceius

Stephanus

Claudius

Marcellus

Lucius

This crossword will really test your Roman knowledge - it's one for experts!

Across

4 A row of columns *(9)*

7 A place where gladiators fought *(12)*

9 Never dying - as the gods were supposed to be *(8)*

10 The centre where business was conducted and meetings took place *(5)*

14 Someone who came from Egypt *(8)*

16 Going on all the time *(9)*

17 Roman poet who wrote the *Metamorphoses* *(4)*

19 A crossword has one! *(4)*

20 A member of one of the tribes who controlled Pompeii before the Romans did *(7)*

21 A city between Syria and Mesopotamia *(7)*

Down

1 Roman city that was destroyed by Vesuvius in AD 79 *(7)*

2 A raised platform round an amphitheatre's arena *(6)*

3 In ancient Rome it may have been a chariot one *(4)*

5 Praising *(9)*

6 Place where the Romans went to bathe *(5)*

8 The second Roman city destroyed by Vesuvius in AD 79 *(11)*

11 The name of the wife of both Mark Antony and Nero *(7)*

12 Fierce and savage, such as the lions in the arena *(9)*

13 The name of Istanbul in ancient times *(9)*

15 The name of the hill in Rome where the Emperor Augustus lived *(8)*

18 For example, Rome or Athens *(4)*

19 The name of the emperor who followed Caracalla *(4)*

Do you know the meanings of these Latin words and phrases?

1 Ad hoc

2 Ad infinitum

3 Etcetera

4 Hic jacet

5 In memoriam

6 Magnum opus

7 Nota bene

8 Post meridiem

9 Pro rata

10 Status quo

11 Tempus fugit

12 Vade mecum

WHAT WAS THE ROMANS' MOST REMARKABLE ACHIEVEMENT?

LEARNING LATIN!

Answers

Page 6 Letter Sums

1. I (1).
2. XII (12).
3. VII (7).
4. V (5).
5. III (3).
6. XXV (25).
7. MCLV (1155).
8. V (5).
9. CCC (300).
10. X (10).

Page 7 At the Forum

There are 10 differences between the two pictures.

Page 8 In the Colosseum

1. 100 *hoplomachae*, 200 *retiarii*, 150 *secutori*, 100 *myrmillii* and 250 *bestiarii*.
2. 15.   3. 44.

Page 9 Lookalikes

Gladiators numbers 3 and 5 are exactly the same.

Page 10 Crossword Primus

Page 12 Emperors All

1. Augustus.
2. Tiberius.
3. Caligula.
4. Caligula.
5. Caracalla.
6. Hadrian.
7. Antoninus Pius.
8. Nero.
9. Constantine.
10. Suetonius, he was a writer.

Page 13 Odd Emperor Out

Statue number 5 is the odd one out.

Page 14 Mountains of Fire

1. Crater (clockwise).
2. Pumice (clockwise).
3. Eruption (anticlockwise).
4. Lava, cone (clockwise).

Page 15 Puzzling Pompeii

Page 16 Imperator!

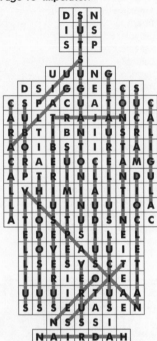

Page 18 Wall-building
1. 3,600.   2. 24.   3. Four weeks.

Page 19 Reverse Order
Picture number 1 shows the correct image.

Page 20 Among the Gods
Apollo - sun.
Ceres - crop-growing.
Diana - hunting.
Juno - queen of the gods.
Jupiter - king of the gods.
Mars - war.
Mercury - messenger of the gods.
Neptune - sea.
Pluto - underworld.
Venus - love.
Vesta - home life.
Vulcan - fire and smithing.

Page 21 Gods Squared
Squares numbers D1 and D6 are the same.

Page 22 Word Muddle
1. Caesar.
2. Emperor.
3. Patrician.
4. Consul.
5. Senator.
6. Plebeian.
7. Amphitheatre.
8. Slave.
9. Latin.
10. Aqueduct.

Page 23 At the Races
There are 63 horses, 21 chariots and 17 charioteers.

Page 24 Crossword Secundus

Page 26 Bath Time
1. c).   2. d).   3. e).   4. f).
5. b).   6. g).   7. h).   8. a).

Page 27 In Hot Water
Things added to the pictures are:
2. Sandal
3. Jug
4. Ointment jar
5. Oil lamp
6. Strigil.

Page 28 **Via Wherea?**

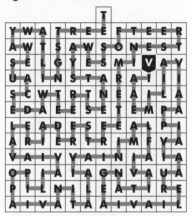

Page 30 **Travelling Problems**

1. Legion A will arrive at 8 p.m. Legion B will arrive at 10 p.m.

2. 29 metres.

3. 282 men. This is how you work it out:

At the end of the first month he has 900 men: 1000 - 100 = 900

At the end of the second month he has 810 men: 900 - 90 = 810

At the end of the third month he has 729 men: 810 - 81 = 729

At the end of the fourth month he has 656 men: 729 - 73 = 656

At the end of the fifth month he has 590 men: 656 - 66 = 590

At the end of the sixth month he has 531 men: 590 - 59 = 531

At the end of the seventh month he has 478 men: 531 - 53 = 478

At the end of the eighth month he has 430 men: 478 - 48 = 430

At the end of the ninth month he has 387 men: 430 - 43 = 387

At the end of the tenth month he has 348 men: 387 - 39 = 348

At the end of the eleventh month he has 313 men: 348 - 35 = 313

At the end of the twelfth month he has 282 men: 313 - 31 = 282

(Note that when working out the 10 per cent you take it to the nearest whole number, thus 10 per cent of 729 is 73.)

Page 31 **On the March**
The following things are wrong with the picture:
Clock, football, 'hamburgerum' sign, satellite dish, road sign, bicycle, traffic lights, chicken, 'dot.com' sign, head-dress, apron, drinks, door, umbrella, trainers, mobile phone, tap.

Page 33 **Caesar's Murder**
Picture number 2 is the correct one.
(Picture 1: bottom left sandal,
Picture 3: stripe on toga,
Picture 4: hairstyle of right-hand figure)

Page 34 **Roman Writers**

1. Livy.
2. Cicero.
3. Horace.
4. Virgil.
5. Ovid.
6. Juvenal.
7. Seneca.
8. Plautus.
9. Catullus.
10. Petronius.
11. Suetonius.
12. Tacitus.

Page 35 **At the Theatre**
There are 25 comic masks and 25 tragic masks.

Page 36 How Many Gladiators?

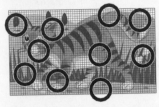

M	O	L	P	O	H	O	P	L	O	M	A
Y	H	O	P	L	O	M	A	C	H	U	S
B	O	R	H	O	P	L	M	S	M	R	U
E	P	U	O	L	L	I	M	U	Y	M	I
S	L	C	T	R	O	R	S	I	R	M	R
T	O	E	H	Y	M	R	M	R	M	Y	A
I	M	S	O	M	A	O	S	A	I	R	I
S	A	U	P	R	C	T	E	I	L	M	T
U	C	I	L	E	H	U	S	T	L	I	E
I	H	R	O	T	U	C	E	S	O	M	R
R	U	A	M	I	S	E	C	E	M	Y	R
A	S	I	A	A	E	S	U	B	Y	R	O
I	E	T	C	R	C	U	T	O	R	M	T
T	C	E	H	I	U	T	O	L	M	I	U
S	U	R	U	U	T	Y	R	L	I	L	C
E	T	R	S	S	O	M	M	I	L	L	E
B	O	Y	M	Y	R	M	I	L	L	O	S

There are four hoplomachae, five secutori, three myrmillii, three retiarii, two bestiarii.

Page 38 True or False?

1. True.
2. False, Augustus was.
3. False, it was Eboracum; Mancunium was Manchester.
4. True.
5. True.
6. False, the coin was called a denarius.
7. True.
8. True.
9. False, they did and had.
10. True.
11. True.
12. False, it was a dining-room.

Page 39 Stone Pictures

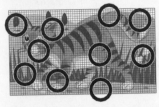

There are 10 differences between the pictures.

Page 40 Crossword Tertius

Page 42 Julian Calendar
Months:
Martius - March.
Maius - May.
Iulius - July.
Augustus - August.
Aprilis - April.
Iunius - June.
Ianuarius - January.
Februarius - February.

Days:
Dies Solis - Sunday.
Dies Lunae - Monday.
Dies Martis - Tuesday.
Dies Mercurii - Wednesday.
Dies Jovis - Thursday.
Dies Veneris - Friday.
Dies Saturni - Saturday.

Page 43 Hour by Hour
Sundials numbers 2, 3 and 6 are the same.

Page 44 Housey, Housey
1. Four.   2. Four.   3. Right.
4. Dog and cat.   5. Two.
6. Second from left.   7. Three.
8. Tiles.   9. Six.   10. Two.

Page 46 Summing Up

1. Incorrect, the answer should be III (3).
2. Incorrect, the answer should be XXI (21).
3. Correct.
4. Incorrect, the answer should be V (5).
5. Correct.
6. Correct.
7. Incorrect, the answer should be III (3).
8. Incorrect, the answer should be LX (60).
9. Correct.
10. Incorrect, the answer should be XXVII (27).

Page 47 E is for Empire . . .

The following things beginning with E are in the picture:
Eagle, Emperor, Entrance, Elf, Eel, Equation, Exit, Ewe, Eland, Elephant, Elk, Effigy, Emu, Easel, Egg, Eye, Ear, and Ear-ring.

Page 48 What's in a Name?

Aqua Arnemetiae - Buxton.
Aquae Sulis - Bath.
Camulodunum - Colchester.
Corinium - Cirencester.
Devana Castra - Chester.
Durnovaria - Dorchester.
Durovernum - Canterbury.
Lindum - Lincoln.
Londinium - London.
Luguvallum - Carlisle.
Maridunum - Carmarthen.
Ratae - Leicester.
Venta Belgarum - Winchester.
Verulanium - St Albans.

Page 49 Founders of Rome

Picture number 3 is different because the wolf has a tooth missing.

Page 50 All That Remains . . .

The endings 'chester' and 'cester' come from the Latin word for 'camp', *castra*.

Page 52 Ladies' Day

1. 49.
2. Three, one of each kind.
3. Wine cost £10.50; olive oil 50p.

Page 53 All Underground

Page 54 Muddled Sentences

1. Rome was founded in 753 BC and its power lasted until AD 476.
2. The Romans used the pound - *libra* - and the ounce - *uncia* - to measure weight.
3. The Roman Republic was set up in 509 BC and continued until the first century BC.
4. The Roman Republic collapsed when Julius Caesar was killed.
5. The three main days of the Roman month were the Calends, the Nones and the Ides.
6. In AD 410 Alaric the Visigoth sacked Rome.
7. The remains of vineyards have been found among the ruins at Pompeii.
8. Roman bathers walked through a foot-bath before entering the swimming pool.
9. Roman shops had large earthenware pots called *dolia* set into their counters.
10. Roman cooking utensils were made of earthenware or bronze.

Page 55 Donkey Work

Marcus is leading Claudius, Stephanus is leading Lucius, Marcellus is leading Ceius.

Page 56 Bumper Crossword

Page 58 All Latin to Me

1. For this special purpose.
2. For ever.
3. And so on.
4. Here lies.
5. In memory of.
6. Great work.
7. Note well.
8. After noon.
9. In proportion.
10. As things are or were.
11. Time flies.
12. Constant companion (it usually mea a favourite book).